STOCK MARKET INVESTING FOR BEGINNERS

Logan Hill

TABLE OF CONTENTS

How frequently have you felt tired of setting off to your work environment practically every day, rain or daylight? Put resources into stocks, and you could be in a situation to sit back at your home with your kids and earn more than your business! Further, imagine the money consequently coming into your financial balance as regularly as you wish! This is nor is an ideal circumstance nor a pipe dream. A great many people over the world are making money sitting at their homes, playing with their kids or traveling on a journey. This is an extremely down to earth situation.

You can turn into a proprietor of a large cross-country organization just by contributing a couple of dollars. You can likewise abandon it if you are not happy with its execution and purchase the stock of some other organization. You can profit as you wish by trading in commodities.

A stock is a breathtaking monetary instrument. It is one of the best devices at any point created to fabricate the wealth of your dreams. Stock trading gives you the money related opportunity that you can never imagine.

If you need to develop rich without the problems that are a particular piece of any business, you should begin trading in stocks. Trading in shares was considered a game of betting just a couple of decades back. To some surviving, maybe, it was. It is no more a bet now. It's anything but a game of visually impaired man's buff or hit and preliminary. It is very nearly a sensible and logical way of earning money. It depends on quick research, investigation and straightforward numerical figurings. What was once considered just an area of the incredibly wealthy has turned into a vehicle for a typical man to wind up a tycoon with tolerance and persistence. Building wealth was never so natural.

When you dispatch your adventure to commercial opportunity by trading in stocks, you should have an intensive comprehension of shares and how they sell on the stock market. Although trading technology has progressed with the development of the stock market, a large portion of the stock traders still doesn't entirely see how to trade stocks. They gather their insight from the easygoing discussion among the visiting bunches where the more significant part of the people themselves don't comprehend what they are discussing.

There are two ways the stock trading is discussed in the dialog bunches around the road corners. One is that Jack has made a fortune by trading in such and such stock since he knows the tricks and tips of the trade. The second remark may contact the other outrageous: Bill has lost his shirt in stock market trading in merely days. The vast majority of this deception comes from the desire to sensationalize the things. There is no uncertainty that stock trading is dangerous and can make and blemish the fortunes, there are ways to make money and secure you against dangers. This should be possible through education about the stock market.

The stock education manufactures the establishment for taking the educated individual choices. You don't need to rely on the tricks and tips that coast around the stock market regularly. Here is some fundamental data:

The ideal way to gain learning in trading is to open a record with a brokerage firm. In any case, before you do that, it is fitting to sign on to the Internet and complete an examination looking for the best brokerage firm. Check the website of each expedite that you run over. Make do with the firm that charges the least brokerage and offers most extreme trading offices.

The website of a decent brokerage firm gives numerous choices to beginners to trade with least dangers of misfortunes. You can earn while you learn and develop bit by bit. The website ought to provide all of you the education required to make you a fruitful expert stock trader.

Peruse through the website of the brokerage firm that interests to you. Contact their customer support service and ask inquiries concerning for what valid reason they ought to be favored over their rivals.

Stock trading technology has made enormous advances. Great stock brokerage firms offer front line advances for trading and research through outlines, constant statements, news flashes, spilling comments and considerably more. They enable you to work at your very own pace and spending plan.

CHAPTER ONE

WHY YOU SHOULD INVEST IN STOCKS

Shares or stocks of a company invariably will, in general, go all over however as time goes on appear to do as such much superior to anything your regular bank account. The fundamental motivation behind why is that each stock inside your investment portfolio can increment or develop in value. For a straightforward model, if a company you have put resources into is doing great, this additionally acknowledges the value of its stocks or shares and along these lines can be sold for all the more making you a benefit.

Then again those of us hoping to make an extra stream of salary can likewise turn towards stocks that payout profit, which is fundamentally month to month or yearly payouts to shareholders.

Presently the original charm of the stock market and contributing must be the opportunity of getting up the right stock, at the right time. Which should be possible with appropriate research and blind luckiness? Putting resources into the market today must be one of the best approaches to construct riches, close by hazard. Now and then any given company, which is by all accounts all good, can experience the ill effects of its industry or sector when request conveys to struggle.

Here is the straightforward kept running down. Regular people or known as retail investors find out about new items or companies in the paper, on TV or the web. Also, having faith in the accomplishment of this item or company starts to put their money through buying stocks. At some point or another specific hindrances become an integral factor that can influence the value of their newly discovered shares, regardless of whether it is war, loan fees or other significant worldwide occasions. What's more, the market starts to endure. Presently the vast majority of these retail investors, who just slapped down several unusual into their first exchanging account, lose the underlying enthusiasm and rapidly sell their current stock portfolios. To spare what little cash they have left. This my companions is an ideal opportunity to buy in! As the market keeps on wallowing and it would seem that the dramatic finish, the brilliant money dependably buys in. What's more, hello following several years the market is back up to where it was again, or we even wind up in another high. The cycle occurs again and again.

Whatever you do, don't give dread or covetousness a chance to show signs of improvement of you. Essentially Buy low, sell high!

TIPS ON WHY YOU SHOULD INVEST IN STOCKS

There is no deficiency of things in which to contribute your money. So why pick stocks? Quietly, because shares are your most solid option. Since its beginning, the stock market has reliably conveyed the best by and large returns when contrasted and the performances of investments like land. Since the motivation behind contributing is to watch your money develop, the intelligent decision is to put your money where it has the most apparent opportunity with regards to doing that.

There are, in any case, moderating conditions and qualities that may influence other investment vehicles to appear to be alluring too. Other investment vehicles you should think about are Bonds, Cash, Mutual funds. When contrasting or thinking about these vehicles as investment choices, know that as their techniques for creating returns vary, in this way, as well, do the only dangers related with every car.

Stocks vs. Bonds

Stocks and bonds go together like nutty spread and jam or macaroni and cheddar. This is intended to infer that to a specific degree you should buy a few relationships. However, on the off chance that you are attempting to settle on buying a share of stock or buying a link, you ought to presumably run with the stock. The return for stock midpoints around 12 percent, while the average yield on a bond is just 5 to 6 percent.

Stocks vs. Cash

Cash, in money-related terms, alludes to an investment that is very fluid. A money market account, for instance, is viewed as cash because the account holder can pull back his or her money without breaking a sweat, including drawing on the report with an individual check. Cash can likewise allude to the funds in your checking and investment accounts or the funds covered up under your sleeping cushion.

Putting resources into stocks will give a higher return than enabling your money to stay in cash or putting it in cash investment. Be that as it may, money has a level of liquidity not offered by stock.

Stocks vs. Mutual Funds

The ongoing ascent in the notoriety of mutual funds has brought them under more extensive and progressively generous examination. Numerous individuals are finding that mutual funds are a fantastic investment alternative, yet stocks are still better.

Stocks naturally give higher returns than mutual funds since the board expenses are not collected on stock proprietors. Mutual funds, be that as it may, offer a higher level of diversification.

Keep in mind, in any case, that the most fundamental explanation behind any investment is to profit. By giving an investment the necessary flexibility to make more significant increases, it ends up fit for making similarly huge misfortunes. This idea is known as "hazard and reward."

10 Reasons Why You Should Invest in Stocks

- **Liquidity:** Because of the liquidity idea of the market, investors can sell their stock whenever they feel, and in three days their check will be prepared.

- **Capital Appreciation:** The share cost will increment in value, and with this, investors are perfect to sell at the rate they so much wish.

- **Bonus And Right Issue:** Investors are regularly rewarded with extra shares at interims while a few companies have a background marked by reward issue like First Bank Plc and right question is the open doors companies provide for shareholders, the right of being a favored buyer of specific rates of their offers.

- **Dividend:** This is the installment of a certain level of the company's yearly returns to the shareholders.

- **Annual General Meeting:** Every investor of companies recorded on the trade is qualified for a sit amid Annual General Meetings.

- **Equity:** There is decency in the market; the puzzling structure of the market takes into account value and reasonableness among each player.

- **Collateral:** Stock investors can utilize their share testament or CSCS Account printout as security for banks or any monetary exchanges, it is legitimate delicate.

- **Flexibility and Diversification:** Stock investment takes into account flexibility and diversification from one sector of the economy to the next.

- **Co-Owner:** Since you are a shareholder in the company you are holding their stock in your portfolio, you have each right like the board on any issue that influences the company or in each advantage.

- **Transferable:** The share purchased by anybody is exchangeable, from one individual to the next; it is even inheritable, that is it very well may be offered on dependants, closest relative or age unborn.

READ THE STOCK MARKET TABLES LIKE A PRO

Stock market news is surrounding us every day in various structures. It's on TV, it's on ticker tapes before commercial buildings, it's in the paper as stock tables, and it's on the internet. So how would you comprehend all the financial information originating from these assets? Learning how to peruse the stock market is a basic necessity for turning into a fruitful investor. Here are the nuts and bolts you need to know.

Step by step instructions to Read the Stock Market Tables

Open any paper to the financial area, and you'll see a table brimming with numbers, bolts, and letters. This is usually a stock table, and it epitomizes the stock market's performance for that day just as gives you past information for the similar investigation.

Albeit each paper's stock tables may be somewhat unique, when all is said in done, they all contain a similar necessary data. Here's the manner by which to peruse the stock market table:

52 week high: This figure gives you the most astounding price for a specific share over the most recent 52 weeks. It's urgent to have the capacity to decide the performance of stock after some time and dissect patterns.

52 week low: This figure will give you the least price for a share over the most recent 52 weeks (about a year). It's likewise essential for assessing patterns and performance. At the point when joined with the 52-week high figure, it should give you an exact appraisal of the stock's yearly production.

Name/Symbol: This segment contains both the company name and its stock symbol. A stock symbol is typically a 3-letter symbol used to recognize the company in the stock market. You have to know the stock symbol of any organizations you put resources into so you can follow their performance after some time and furthermore when you utilize the internet to discover stock statements. Organizations frequently pick important ticker symbols, so for instance, Genentech, a biotechnology firm, has the stock symbol DNA.

Profit: The sum paid on a yearly premise by a company as a benefit to its shareholders.

Volume: The number of shares exchanged today for a specific stock.

Yield: Yield is a rate determined as profit partitioned by stock price; the return of a specific stock may change consistently relying upon its stock price for that day.

P/E Ratio: This ratio is just the price of stock partitioned by the company's profit per share. When all is said in done a lower P/E ratio is attractive because it would imply that the company is decent esteem speculation at the current cost.

Day Last: This would be today's stock price, or at whatever point the stock keep going exchanged on a business day.

Net Change: The net change estimates the differential in the stock price between its current price and the price the prior day, and reports the move as a rate.

The most effective method to Read the Stock Market Ticker Tape

The stock market ticker tape keeps running on TV channels, just as outside financial buildings and the Internet. It's generally a quick look at how different stocks are performing on the current day. It signifies stocks by their symbol, which can be somewhere in the range of one to four letters. A few organizations condense their business name, so Google's logo is GOOG, while different organizations utilize their whole name, for example, NIKE.

The ticker for the most part additionally demonstrates either a green bolt, showing increment in stock price, or a red bolt demonstrating a decline in stock price pursued by a rate figure indicating the measure of change in stock price for the day's trading.

Both stock tables and stock tickers are useful for an investor to screen and track stock performance. Realizing how to peruse the stock market is significant for any investor since stock investing is tied in with making and afterward checking your speculation so you can change your stock portfolio to ideal market conditions.

Stock Market Basics - Do You Want to Become a Professional Investor?

People need to get into the stock market trading since they like to gain a great deal of cash. Data about normal individuals acquiring a ton in just a single day grabs their eye to do the precisely the equivalent. Numerous individuals only need to deliver a few additional dollars. For whatever reason that could be, 99% of the individuals who genuinely need to learn and comprehend about stocks haven't any thought of where to begin. Regularly, they'd end up getting lost with the tremendous volume of data accessible on the web.

The goal of this part is to help you in learning how you can do stock trading in the best possible way. As in any other exchange, Stock trading has a significant learning bend however if you have quality information accessible, this bend will be shorter.

In case you suppose to get into a confounded internet webpage immediately, you will have a significant shock because shockingly your first site should be tied in with learning about the stock market basics to start connecting with investing vocabulary.

Unquestionably you initially need to comprehend what you're doing, and this will take some time. Time is its quintessence and each additional time must be engaged to research, read and watch everything on the stock market for tenderfoots.

If you are not set up to do this, the stock market isn't for you. Take a great deal of time considering and learning, and soon you will be astounded with how much data you honestly have.

You should scan for associations that put out day by day points of view when you see stock market basics. You will probably find information that may potentially send the expense of a stock or share up or down.

Stock investing is extremely hard first of all since they wouldn't understand when to stop and to accept benefit or misfortune as talented investors would do. Sometimes, beginners don't haul out quick when they lose, however, endeavor to ride out the storm and drop more. These are the elements of why you should examine the basics of investing in the stock business.

LEADING PENNY STOCK INVESTMENTS - HOW TO FIND THEM

People are continually searching for the main penny stock investments. This is typically the primary objective of people putting resources into penny stocks. If they find them, they will profit snappy. The issue is a great many people don't have the experience, and contributing information to find these beneficial stocks. The more significant part of people see penny stocks as a make easy money opportunity; they provide their money aimlessly dependent on hunches then they end up losing their money. The 20/80 rule happens in penny stocks. This implies 20% of investors have 80% of the riches. So are we going to find the main penny stock investments?

As a matter of first importance, you should be clever as you can and invest a great deal of energy looking into. A few apparatuses that active investors use is stock newsletters. You buy into one of these, and usually about once every week they will send you stock picks. These newsletters are gold, and they will increase your prosperity rate. They are sponsored by vast amounts of research and information and are an extremely significant asset. Notwithstanding, when you get your stock picks I propose completing a smidgen of research before you put resources into one these driving penny stock investments.

While stock newsletters are a suitable instrument, stock picking programming is lovely. If you will utilize one way and one path to pick your stocks, this is your most solid option. These projects can outflank any human personality with regards to investigating. They can break down several stocks every moment, and with this information, they can foresee which shares will be painful. These projects will give you precise stocks picks 4/5 times. In penny stocks anything over half is incredible. This is the ideal approach to find the main penny stock investments.

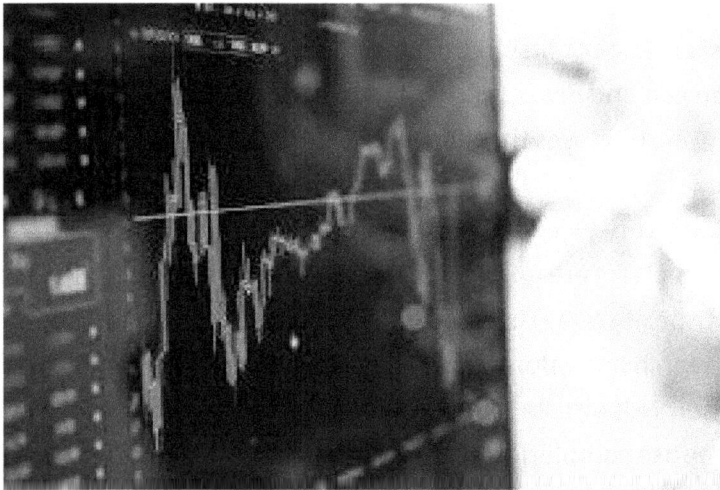

CHAPTER TWO

SIX KEYS TO FIND MOMENTUM STOCKS

Momentum stock exchange has been around for a little while and has been demonstrated to a sound technique for making fabulous riches in the stock market. Amid the 1990s, for instance, Clear Channel Communications went up 5,615%, Emulex rose 6,412%, Dell Computer went up 10,198%, Activision went up 13,819%, and Semtech rose 15,231%.

It isn't unprecedented to find stocks that quicken in price that proceed to make 100% to 300% returns in under a year or even in a couple of months. Be that as it may, for starting investors it tends to be a befuddling and baffling background to find such stocks.

While numerous momentum stock brokers all have different criteria while looking out tomorrow's huge champs, there are regularly six key advances when screening for a primary victor.

They are:

1) Accelerating earnings or EPS (earnings per share).

2)Annual earnings up 25% or more over the most recent three years.

3)The minimum volume of 100,000 or possibly expanding amount.

4) A 17% ROE (return on value) or better.

5) Has the position of authority in the market place.

6) Price at a record-breaking high.

Potential stocks for momentum exchanging should show solid basics on their financial record and show that they are growing at a quickened rate. By choosing stocks that are showing high EPS evaluations and accelerating rates of development over past quarters you can make sure that you have an organization that is growing out a better than expected rate. Money Street cherishes earnings that are increasing and an organization that will be rewarded with institutional sponsorship by the enormous subsidies further causing share value to rise.

Momentum stocks additionally have shown that they are solid players in their market and demonstrate there value by displaying solid annual earnings. Not exactly a 25% yearly increase in yearly revenues won't animate enthusiasm by the enormous common assets or investors bringing about a stock whose price will probably stay dormant or increase in value at too moderate a pace for momentum contributing.

Stocks for thought ought to have day by day normal of 100,000 shares or possibly observe there standard everyday volume increase as the value of the stock ascents. Any volume not as much as this shows little enthusiasm by the investment network and you could find yourself experiencing difficulty with liquidity in the stock if you have to move and get out.

A potential stock should show an ROE of 17% or better. ROE is the net gain partitioned by the number of shares held by investors. It shows the mindful profit for capital by investors and the higher this proportion is, the better for investors. As I would like to think, this is a standout amongst the essential properties for any stock investment.

Momentum stocks are additionally pioneers in the market. At the point when the critical files have decreased, genuine stock pioneers display quality by holding or notwithstanding surpassing their highs or close there tops. At the end when the real records rally these pioneers usually lead the rally and proceed to make new highs and outpace the market.

Momentum stocks ought to likewise be exchanged at there unsurpassed highs. Purchase transferring at these dimensions at essential specific section guides you are likely to ride the trend as the stock increases in share price. This kind of trademark increases your odds for gainfulness because an up direction in place is six times bound to remain in place, so you have the chances on your side.

You can stock for sweeps like these at Yahoo Financial or MSN Financial for nothing. Start keeping a rundown of potential applicants and after that track there execution. It might take a little practice however with time you will have the capacity to detect the stocks that proceed to make the vast moves of 100% or more.

Similarly as with a wide range of putting remember to cut your washouts rapidly and ride your champs with decent money the board plan.

HOW TO TRADE STOCKS ONLINE

There are two diverse ways that you can trade stocks and make money in this endeavor - you buy stocks on the trading floor, or you can buy online. With the convenience of purchasing and selling shares at the solaces of your own home, or wherever you are, stock trading online has turned out to be well known. It is one reason that many average folks are currently additionally making money in stock trading.

If you need to learn how to trade stocks online, you can discover a lot of assets, yet you can start with the nuts and bolts. Before going into the genuine joining or contributing your money, here are a couple of things that you ought to consider and get ready.

- Learn the phrasings and everything about stock trading. Try not to go trading if you don't have the foggiest idea about the terms utilized in trading. A 'bear' and a 'bull' is regularly referenced in stock trading and don't make yourself ponder what a bear and a bull are doing in the stock market. Continuously learn the phrasings are previously trading.

- **Ready your instruments.** Heading off to this unsafe clash of purchasing and selling stocks with no devices within reach can twofold and triple your danger of losing more, so make beyond any doubt you have your instruments with you. Additionally, make beyond any doubt you have done your examination, you have outlines and diagrams to enable you to dissect the stock market, and you have decent programming that will allow you to put a few tasks in autopilot. Without a doubt, nowadays, you don't need to do everything physically. By utilizing the product to do a few chores, you will have more opportunity to concentrate on your system and have all the more spare time too.

If you are prepared and resolved to make benefits out of stock trading, here are the first strides on the most proficient method to trade stocks online.

1. Locate a decent broker. Make beyond any doubt the broker you have picked is reliable and has conclusively settled a decent record with regards to online stock trading. You would need to have a broker who can remain by you with regards to achieving your objectives in stock trading. Make beyond any doubt they have reasonable expenses also.

2. Have your very own trading system. Make beyond any doubt it does work and make sure to adhere to that system when trading. One key to being useful in trading stocks is to comply with a policy that works and not merely buying with the surge of your feelings.

3. Sign for an application. Get the structures and archives from your broker. You will at that point choose what kind of account you need to open. Get some information about the choices you have.

4. Reserve your account. In the wake of marking off a few records and upon endorsement, you may then reserve your account. Remember too that distinctive brokerage may have different essentials. Another essential hint on the best way to trade stocks online that you ought to always remember is to contribute just an amount that you are happy to lose. The dissatisfaction and frustration in losing everything you have can be challenging to manage, so make beyond any doubt you contribute admirably.

5. Start trading. Bear in mind dependably that when you start to buy, there can be benefits and loses however dependably keep your order perfect. Realize when to state No to stay away from much loses. Active traders are for the most part trained ones.

Learn more tips and traps on the most proficient method to trade stocks online, and without a doubt, you will make great money out of it in no time.

LEARN HOW TO TRADE STOCKS ONLINE

As innovation keeps on growing, so does the thriving online stock trading business. Online stock trading is currently simpler than at any other time. You would now be able to learn how to trade stocks online effectively. If you have any related knowledge in stock trading, online stock trading ought to be extremely basic. Besides convenience, online stock trading has numerous different advantages.

After you have settled on the choice to trade online, at that point, you should decide if you need to manage long haul or present moment investments. You can make the most proportion of money at all amount of time by choosing to day-trade. Day-trading is best for the individuals who have probably some speculation experience. This method isn't suggested for fledgling traders. You will require skill to appropriately day-trade. New speculators, who don't yet totally get a handle on the most proficient method to trade stocks online, should stick to extended haul trading.

To start online trading, you should have an account with an online brokerage. When you have figured out what sort of trading you need to do, you should make a statement with your preferred online trading administration. It tends to be hard to pick the correct site for you, yet by investing energy doing exploration and remembering a couple of important things, you will have the capacity to locate the ideal place for you.

You should think about whether the online administration offers swing trading, day trading, or both. You should consider regardless of whether the brokerage offers money the board preparing. Investigate the site itself. Is it easy to understand? Does the site offer advice on methodologies? You ought to likewise consider the age of the organization.

If you need convenience and reasonable costs, online stock trading is for you. Regardless of whether you are uncertain how to trade stocks online, the online method is preferable for learners over the conventional manner. Online stock trading organizations offer essential advice and instructional exercises, with the goal that your inquiries will be replied and you can rapidly learn all you have to know. These organizations additionally have specialists close by to enable you to design your methodology.

A champion among the most important things you have to think about while picking an online stock brokerage is security. The dimension of security the site gives is essential. If the place isn't anchor, you are putting your well-deserved money in danger. You ought to likewise make sure to experiment with any item you plan on utilizing. Most quality online brokerages will offer a preliminary bundle.

When you have decided the kind of trading you needed to do and picked a stable and secure online brokerage firm; you are prepared to start contributing. Make sure to pursue this basic advice, and you will learn how to trade stocks online like a genius.

Federal or state securities laws require brokers, advisers, and their firms to be licensed or registered, and to make important information public. But it's up to you to find that information and use it to protect your investment dollars. The good news is this information is easy to get, and one phone call or web search may save you from sending your money to a con artist, a bad broker, or disreputable firm.

This is very important, because if you do business with an unlicensed securities broker or a firm that later goes out of business, there may be no way for you to recover your money even if an arbitrator or court rules in your favor.

BROKERS AND BROKERAGE FIRMS

The Central Registration Depository (or "CRD") is a computerized database that contains information about most brokers, their representatives, and the firms they work for. For instance, you can find out if brokers are properly licensed in your state and if they have had run-ins with regulators or received serious complaints from investors. You'll also find information about the brokers' educational backgrounds and where they've worked before their current jobs.

You can ask either your State Securities Regulator or NASD to provide you with information from the CRD. Your State Securities Regulator may provide more information from the CRD than NASD, especially when it comes to investor complaints, so you may want to check with them first. You'll find contact information for your State Securities Regulator on the North American Securities Administrators Association

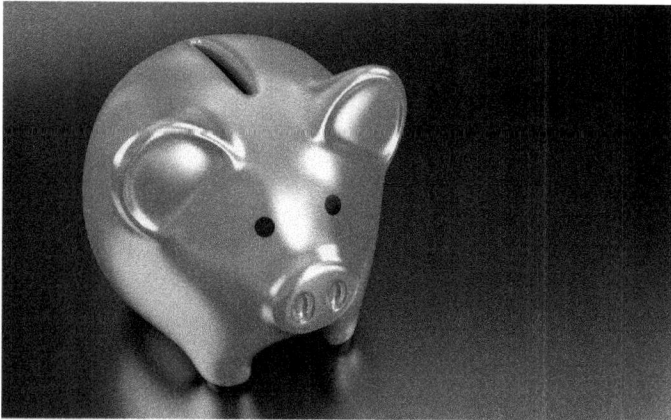

INVESTMENT ADVISERS

People or firms that get paid to give advice about investing in securities must register with either the U.S. Securities and Exchange Commission (SEC) or the State Securities Regulator where they have their principal place of business. Investment advisers who manage $25 million or more in client assets generally must register with the SEC. If they manage less than $25 million, they generally must register with the State Securities Regulator

Some investment advisers employ investment adviser representatives, the people who actually work with clients. In most cases, these people must be licensed or registered with your State Securities Regulator to do business with you. So be sure to check them out.

To find out about advisers and whether they are properly registered, read their registration forms, called the "Form ADV," which has two parts. Part 1 has information about the adviser's business and whether they've had problems with regulators or clients. Part 2 outlines the adviser's services, fees and strategies. Before you hire an investment adviser, always ask for and carefully read both parts of the ADV.

You can view an adviser's most recent Form ADV online. The database contains Forms ADV only for investment adviser firms that register electronically using the Investment Adviser Registration Depository, but will expand to encompass all registered investment advisers—individuals as well as firms.

CHAPTER THREE

DIFFERENT TYPES OF STOCKS

First it's important to understand what a stock is. When investors talk about stocks, they usually mean ⊛common" stocks. A share of common stock represents a share of ownership in the company that issues it. The price of the stock goes up and down, depending on how the company performs and how investors think the company will perform in the future. The stock may or may not pay dividends, which usually come from profits. If profits fall, dividend payments may be cut or eliminated.

Many companies also issue "preferred" stock. Like common stock, it is a share of ownership. The difference is preferred stockholders get first dibs on dividends in good times and on assets if the company goes broke and has to liquidate.

Theoretically, the price of preferred stock can rise or fall along with the common. In reality it doesn't move nearly as much because preferred investors are interested mainly in the dividends, which are fixed when the stock is issued. For this reason, preferred stock is more comparable to a bond than to a share of common stock.

It's hard to think of a compelling reason to buy preferred stocks. They generally pay a slightly lower yield than the same company's bonds and are no safer. Their potential equity kicker (the chance that the preferred will rise in price along with the common stock) has been largely illusory. Preferred stock is really better suited for corporate portfolios because a corporation doesn't have to pay federal income tax on most of the dividends it receives from another corporation.

Stocks are bought and sold on one or more of several "stock markets," the best known of which are the New York Stock Exchange (NYSE), the American Stock Exchange (AMEX), and Nasdaq. There are also several regional exchanges, ranging from Boston to Honolulu. Stocks sold on an exchange are said to be "listed" there; stocks sold through Nasdaq may be called "over-the-counter" (OTC) stocks

GROWTH STOCKS have good prospects for growing faster than the economy or the stock market in general and in general are average to above average risk. Investors buy them because of their good record of earnings growth and the expectation that they will continue generating capital gains over the long term.

BLUE-CHIP STOCKS won't be found on an official "Blue Chip Stock" list. Blue- chip stocks are generally industry-leading companies with top-shelf financial credentials. They tend to pay decent, steadily rising dividends, generate some growth, offer safety and reliability. and are low-to-moderate risk. These stocks can form your retirement portfolio's core holdings a grouping of stocks you plan to hold "forever," while adding other investments to your portfolio.

INCOME STOCKS pay out a much larger portion of their profits (often 50% to 80%) in the form of quarterly dividends than do other stocks. These tend to be more mature, slower-growth companies, and the dividends paid to investors make these shares generally less risky to own than shares of growth or small-company stocks. Though share prices of income stocks aren't expected to grow rapidly, the dividend acts as a kind of cushion beneath the share price. Even if the market in general falls, income stocks are usually less affected because investors will still receive the dividend.

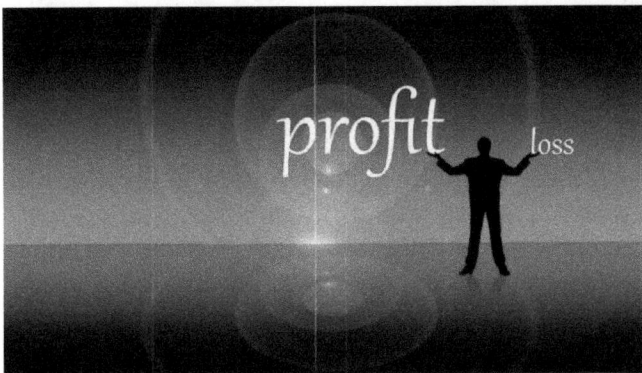

DEFENSIVE STOCKS are theoretically insulated from the business cycle (and there- fore lower in risk) because people go right on buying their products and services in bad times as well as good. Utility companies fit here (another overlap), as do companies that sell food, beverages and drugs.

VALUE STOCKS earn the name when they are considered underpriced according to several measures of value described later in this booklet. A stock with an unusually low price in relation to the company's earnings may be dubbed a "value stock" if it exhibits other signs of good health. Risk here can vary greatly.

SPECULATIVE STOCKS may be unproven young dot-coms or erratic or down-at- the-heels old companies exhibiting some sort of spark, such as the promise of an imminent technological breakthrough or a brilliant new chief executive. Buyers of speculative stocks have hopes of making big profits. Most speculative stocks don't do well in the long run, so it takes big gains in a few to offset your losses in the many. Risk here, no surprise, is high.

CYCLICAL STOCKS are called that because their fortunes tend to rise and fall with those of the economy at large, prospering when the business cycle is on the upswing, suffering in recessions. Automobile manufacturers are a prime example, which illustrates the important fact that these categories often overlap. Other industries whose profits are sensitive to the business cycle include airlines, steel, chemicals and businesses dependent on home building.

Now that you know the characteristics of good stocks, you have to address the question of how to go about buying them. One of the biggest worries is timing. Suppose you're unlucky enough to buy at the very top of the market? Or suppose something unexpected happens to dash the price of your shares overnight? How can you protect yourself against bad things happening to good stocks while you're holding a basketful of them?

46

Dollar-cost averaging is a time-tested method of smoothing out the roller-coaster ride that awaits those who try to time the market. You don't have to be brilliant to make dollar-cost averaging work, and you don't even have to pay especially close attention to what's happening in the stock market or in economy. With dollar-cost averaging, you simply invest a fixed amount regularly, depending on your saving schedule. The key is to keep to your schedule, regardless of whether stock prices go up or down.

Because you're investing a fixed amount at fixed intervals, your dollars buy more shares when prices are low. As a result, the average purchase price of your stock will usually be lower than the average of the market prices over the same time.

Here's an example of how dollar cost averaging usually works. Say you invest $300 a month over a six-month period in Acme Enterprises, a stock that ranges in price from a low of $20 to a high of $30. Here's a look at what dollar-cost averaging would do. (This example ignores brokerage commissions.)

THIRD MONTH: Things have stabilized. The price of your stocks is still $25, and you buy another 12 shares.

FOURTH MONTH: On news of a takeover bid by another company, the price soars to $33. Your $300 buys you only nine shares, with a little change left over.

FIFTH MONTH: The takeover bid falls through and the price dips back down to $25. You pick up another 12 shares.

SIXTH MONTH: An earnings report that falls short of analysts' expectations causes a couple of mutual funds to sell your stock, pushing the price down to $20 a share. You acquire 15 shares.

LET'S ADD IT UP: So far you've spent, in round numbers, $1,800 (not counting commissions) and you own 70 shares of Acme, which means you paid an average of $25.71 a share. Compare that with other ways you could have acquired the stock: If you had bought ten shares during each of those six months, you'd own 60 shares at an average price per share of $26.33. If you had invested the entire $1,800 at the start of the period, you'd own 60 shares at $30 per share. You can begin to see the advantages of dollar-cost averaging.

Now, you might have noticed that at the end of the sixth month you were holding stock for which you had paid an average price of nearly $26 in a market that was willing to pay you only $20 a share. What now? Should you sell and cut your losses? Not necessarily. Now is a good time to reassess your faith in Acme; reexamine the fundamentals described earlier. If the fundamentals still justify your faith, this dip in the price represents a good opportunity to buy more shares.

Dollar-cost averaging won't automatically improve the performance of your portfolio. But don't underestimate the value of the added discipline, organization and peace of mind it gives you. It's natural to be frightened away from owning stocks when prices head down, even though experience has shown that such times can be the best time to buy.

Although dollar-cost averaging lets you put your investments on autopilot, you shouldn't leave them there indefinitely. Inflation and increases in your salary make your fixed-dollar contribution less meaningful over time, and you shouldn't continue to buy any stock merely out of habit. Reexamine the company's investment prospects on a regular schedule—at least once a year—and adjust your investment accordingly.

REINVESTING YOUR DIVIDENDS

Another investment strategy that, like dollar-cost averaging, pays little attention to the direction of prices uses corporate dividends to boost profits over the long term. It's called the direct investment plan, dividend reinvestment plan, or DRIP. More than 1,300 companies offer these special programs. Instead of sending you a check

Another investment strategy that, like dollar-cost averaging, pays little attention to the direction of prices uses corporate dividends to boost profits over the long term. It's called the direct investment plan, dividend reinvestment plan, or DRIP. More than 1,300 companies offer these special programs. Instead of sending you a check

DRIPs have other advantages:

> **Small dividends buy fractional shares**, a help to small investors.

> **Many DRIPs let you make additional investments** on your own. In addition, a handful of companies allow you to buy more shares with your dividends, sometimes even offering DRIP shares at dis- counts of 3% to 5% from the market price.

> **You reduce risk** by investing via a DRIP because it's a form of dollar-cost averaging.

> **Some plans charge small fees**, such as a maximum $2.50 administrative fee per transaction, or $1 to $15 if you want possession of stock certificates. Brokers who hold stocks that are in a DRIP charge little or nothing to add these shares to your account each dividend period.

HOW YOU JOIN. Joining a DRIP is easy. Just check the company's Web site or call its shareholder relations department for a prospectus and an application, and send back the completed form. Often, you must already own some stock before you can sign up.

You'll probably have to buy your first shares through a broker, register the stock in your own name (not in the broker's "street" name), and then transfer it to the DRIP. A small but growing number of companies will handle an initial purchase directly.

HOW YOU GET OUT. DRIPs can pose a problem when it's time to sell. Since most DRIP investors are long-termers, companies are not geared toward sales. It used to take weeks to get your money, but things are getting a little better. Many DRIP plans now purchase shares weekly or even daily; some even permit investors to sell their shares via the telephone. In some cases you need only write a letter stating the number of shares that you wish to sell, and the company will send you the proceeds. But other companies merely mail you a stock certificate, which you must then sell through a broker. A few firms also limit selling to specified amounts, such as 100- share lots.

If you don't plan to hold the stock for at least five years, a DRIP may not be for you. Remembering the rules of each plan can be confusing if you belong to several, and there's no guarantee those rules won't change. You may be limited to buying additional shares only at monthly or quarterly intervals that coincide with dividend payment dates. Money for voluntary cash purchases is often held by the company— at no interest—until the plan's purchase dates.

All reinvested dividends are taxable for the year they're paid, even though you don't see the money. And if the shares were bought at a discount from the market, the amount of the discount is included in your taxable income in the year of purchase.

HOW TO PICK A DRIP. Don't buy a stock just because it offers a direct investment plan. Evaluate the company's fundamentals, as described earlier, and consider the following points:

Check the limits if you plan to invest additional cash through a DRIP. Some companies will let you contribute as little as $10 per month. Others have higher mini- mums. Nearly all have maximums, ranging from $1,000 to more than $5,000 per month. Plans with the lowest minimums will be more attractive to small investors. Ask for the company's dividend record dates—when dividends are recorded on the books. By sending voluntary payments just before the record date you can cut down on waiting time for reinvestment. The same applies when you first sign up.

Check the prospectus. A few plans let you receive part of your dividends in cash and have part reinvested.

DIRECT-PURCHASE, OR NO-LOAD PLANS. While there are hundreds of no-fee DRIPs still available, the trend has been away from them. The plans that are displacing many DRIPs offer some of the features that have made mutual funds so popular. Most retain the dividend-reinvestment option but allow investors to avoid brokerage fees entirely by purchasing even the first share of stock directly from the company. These plans are called direct-purchase plans (DPPs), or no-load stocks.

Most plans allow investors to make additional cash purchases on a weekly or monthly schedule via electronic debiting of their bank account. Some even allow you to set up an individual retirement account (IRA) or sell shares over the phone. A few offer discounts on the price of the stock and allow participants to borrow against the value of their shares, as they would with a margin account at a brokerage.

If the market's a similar thing is valid. You can make vast amounts of money on the long side while your short positions are getting injured.

This encourages you to make money regardless of which way the markets might head. This procedure is particularly essential amid sideways markets. In these conditions, stocks can head up 100 one day and crash 200 the

following. If you were diversified among long and short positions, you could make money regardless of what occurs in the market. Something else you should take a gander at is exchanging more towards the side of the market. At the end of the day, if the markets are incredibly bullish, you ought to most likely have increasingly bullish trades then bearish open. If they are bearish you ought to have increasingly bearish trades', bullish open. Regardless you need to grow long and short exchanging frameworks that work. If your short term trades are not working now, they presumably won't work if you do broaden.

INVESTMENT PROFESSIONAL

Are you the type of person who will read as much as possible about potential investments and ask questions about them? If so, maybe you don't need investment advice.

But if you're busy with your job, your children, or other responsibilities, or feel you don't know enough about investing on your own, then you may need some help.

Brokers and investment advisers offer a variety of services at a variety of prices. It pays to comparison shop.

You can get investment advice from most financial institutions that sell investments, including brokerages, banks, mutual fund companies, and insurance companies. You can also hire a broker, an investment adviser, an accountant, or a financial planner to help you make investment decisions.
There is no such thing as a free lunch. Investment advisers and brokers do not perform their services as an act of charity. If they are working for you, they are getting paid for their efforts.

Some of their fees are easier to see immediately than are others. But, in all cases, you should always feel free to ask questions about how and how much your adviser is being paid. And if the fee is quoted to you as a percentage, make sure that you understand what that translates to in dollars.

Tricky Titles

If a broker or adviser has initials after his name, don't assume that makes that individual better qualified than another. These titles are not all the same and do not necessarily mean better service for you. In fact, the initials may mean that the adviser or broker can only sell certain products. Check the titles to see if there are limits on what that adviser or broker can sell. For instance, if someone can only sell fixed annuities, he or she may be inclined to recommend them for every customer.

Must Read Tip

If you have a brokerage account, read your statement every month -- it may not be fun to look at it when the market is down, but it is your most important protection against unauthorized transactions. If you do not object in writing within ten days of receiving notification of a transaction, you might not be able to contest it later. That's why it's important to read your statement and object right away if something is wrong

ONLINE INVESTING

Online trading is quick and easy, but online investing takes time. With the click of a mouse, you can buy and sell stocks from one of the many online brokers offering low-cost trades. Although online trading saves investors time and money, it does not take the homework out of making investment decisions. You may be able to make a fast trade, but making wise investment decisions takes time. Before you trade, know why you are buying or selling, and the risk of your investment.

Set Your Price Limits

To avoid buying or selling a stock at a price higher or lower than you wanted, you should place a limit order rather than a market order. A limit order is an order to buy or sell a security at a specific price. A buy limit order can only be executed at the limit price or lower, and a sell limit order can only be executed at the limit price or higher. Your limit order will not be executed if the market price quickly surpasses your limit before your order can be filled. But, by using a limit order, you protect yourself from buying the stock at too high a price or selling it at too low a price.

If You Place An Order, Check To Make Sure It Was Executed

Some investors mistakenly assume that their orders have not been executed and place the order again. They end up buying or selling twice, which can be a costly mistake. Talk with your financial services firm about how you should handle a situation where you are unsure if your original order was executed.

If You Cancel An Order, Make Sure The Cancellation Worked Before Placing Another Trade

When you cancel an online trade, make sure that your original transaction was not executed. Although you may receive an electronic receipt for the cancellation, don't assume the trade was cancelled. Orders can only be cancelled if they have not been executed. Ask your financial services firm about how you can confirm that a cancellation order worked.

If You Purchase A Security In A Cash Account, You Must Pay For It Before You Can Sell It

In a cash account, you must pay for the purchase of a stock before you sell it. If you buy and sell a stock before paying for it, you are freeriding. Freeriding violates the credit extension provisions of the Federal Reserve Board's Regulation T.

Diversifying your portfolio can be a hugely successful approach to trade in the stock exchange. It can enable you to spread your money over a wide range of changes that can help increment your odds of achievement. It will likewise help with hazard the executives. By not having the majority of your record into one trade you will be less influenced if that trade does not turn out the manner in which you need it to. The thing that a great many people don't consider with expansion is diversifying with both long and short positions. Numerous traders loathe bears and sideways markets. They are a strict bull. With the end goal for them to be all around diversified as traders, they ought to have probably a type of bearish trades going on even while they have bullish trades. The explanation for this is you are shielded from astonishments in the market. If the market crashes, your Bullish positions will likely get smashed your bearish positions however will do superbly and ideally more than make up for the misfortunes you went up against the long side

Disclaimer Statement

All information and content contained in this book are provided solely for general information and reference purposes. Smith Show Publishing LLC Limited makes no statement, representation, warranty or guarantee as to the accuracy, reliability or timeliness of the information and content contained in this Book.

Neither Smith Show Publishing Limited or the author of this book nor any of its related company accepts any responsibility or liability for any direct or indirect loss or damage (whether in tort, contract or otherwise) which may be suffered or occasioned by any person howsoever arising due to any inaccuracy, omission, misrepresentation or error in respect of any information and content provided by this book (including any third-party books.

notes

notes

notes

notes

notes

notes

notes

notes

notes